Jeden Tag ein bisschen besser

ENGLISCH

6. Schuljahr

von
Ingrid Preedy
Brigitte Seidl

Illustriert von
Roland Beier

Cornelsen
SCRIPTOR

Die Autorinnen:
Ingrid Preedy ist Britin. Sie hat langjährige Erfahrung als Englischlehrerin und ist in der Lehrerfortbildung tätig. Sie ist Autorin mehrerer Schulbücher und Unterrichtsmaterialien.
Brigitte Seidl verfügt über 20jährige Berufserfahrung als Englisch-, Deutsch- und Sportlehrerin. Auch sie ist Autorin mehrerer Lehrwerke und Unterrichtsmaterialien.

Cornelsen online http://www.cornelsen.de

Gedruckt auf chlorfrei gebleichtem Papier
ohne Dioxinbelastung der Gewässer.

Bibliografische Information
Die Deutsche Bibliothek verzeichnet diese Publikation in der Deutschen Nationalbibliografie; detaillierte bibliografische Daten sind im Internet über **http://dnb.ddb.de** abrufbar.

Dieses Werk berücksichtigt die Regeln der reformierten Rechtschreibung und Zeichensetzung.

7. 6. 5. 4. € Die letzten Ziffern bezeichnen
07 06 05 04 Zahl und Jahr der Auflage.

Redaktion: Gregor Rauh, Berlin
Typographie: Julia Walch, Bad Soden
Illustrationen: Roland Beier, Berlin
Umschlagentwurf: Vera Bauer, Berlin,
unter Verwendung einer Illustration von Roland Beier
Layout: Beate Schubert, Berlin
Druck und Bindearbeiten: Clausen & Bosse, Leck
Printed in Germany
ISBN 3-589-21197-0
Bestellnummer 211970

Inhalt

Vorwort

Hallo, liebe Schülerinnen und Schüler!

Hallo, liebe Eltern!

Wer ***jeden Tag ein bisschen besser*** wird, ist bald sehr gut!

Dieses Heft stellt auf jeder Doppelseite ein Thema aus dem Englischunterricht der 6. Klasse vor, das in einer Viertel- oder einer halben Stunde bearbeitet werden kann. Eine Doppelseite pro Tag genügt völlig.
Man schreibt einfach direkt ins Heft rein. Ist einmal nicht genug Platz, kann auch alles auf ein Blatt Papier geschrieben werden.

In der Mitte des Heftes haben wir einen Lösungsteil zum Heraustrennen eingeheftet. Damit sollen immer gleich die Ergebnisse überprüft werden! Das ist ganz wichtig, um in Zukunft Fehler zu vermeiden!

Viel Spaß und viel Erfolg!

1 English words in German

Das Datum von heute

____

Working with a dictionary

Gerade eben ist ein Spaceshuttle vom Mars auf der Erde gelandet. Bevor die Crew ihr Raumschiff verlassen kann, muss sie noch einen kurzen Check bei folgenden Geräten vornehmen: Ist der Airbag in Ordnung? Empfängt der Receiver noch alle Funksignale? Ist das Handy eingeschaltet? Bootet der Computer? Ist eine E-mail angekommen?
Schließlich öffnet sich langsam eine Tür, und zwei Aliens betreten den Erdboden. Sie sind echt groggy. Ihnen war schon beim Take-off etwas mulmig gewesen. Dabei hatten sie sich vorher mit Fahrten auf ihren Mountainbikes, mit Jogging und mit Bodybuilding für die anstrengende Reise fit gehalten.
Die Kids finden die beiden in ihren Moonboots und Kingsize-Overalls ziemlich cool.

In der deutschen Sprache werden viele englische Worte benutzt.
Oft bedeuten die Worte ursprünglich im Englischen etwas anderes als jetzt im Deutschen.
Ein Beispiel: Im Englischen gibt es das Wort *handy* nur als Adjektiv und hat drei Bedeutungen: 1. praktisch/nützlich, 2. griffbereit, 3. geschickt.
Im Deutschen gibt es „das Handy" nur als Substantiv und bezeichnet ein schnurloses Funktelefon.

Der Text enthält 21 Worte, die aus dem Englischen übernommen wurden. Kennst du sie alle? Schreibe sie der Reihe nach aus dem Text heraus.

A B C D E F G H I J K L M N O P Q R S T U V W X Y Z

Ordne die Worte alphabetisch (siehe rechter Seitenrand) in die nummerierten, linken Spalten. Schlage sie dann im Wörterbuch nach.
Oft musst du Wortteile nachschlagen (z. B. *moonboots* ➔ *moon* und *boots*).
Schreibe die Bedeutungen, die du im Wörterbuch findest, in die rechte Spalte.

1.	Airbag	Luftsack	12.		
2.			13.		
3.			14.		
4.			15.		
5.			16.		
6.			17.		
7.			18.		
8.			19.		
9.			20.		
10.			21.		
11.					

2 What a birthday

Das Datum von heute

Simple past-statements with regular and irregular verbs

In den Geschenken kannst du lesen, was an Janes Geburtstag los war. Aber die Textteile sind in der ganz falschen Reihenfolge. Nummeriere sie an den Geschenkanhängern richtig durch.

They play games. In one game Tom turns off the light and tries to catch the other children. Suddenly he falls over something. He lies on the floor. He can't get up.

Then Jane's mother turns on the light again. The children can't see Tom. Where is he? Then Jane sees Tom under the table with Maxi, her dog.

At eight o'clock the party is over. The children go home and Jane goes to her room.

Tom has something in his hand. It's a piece of cake. But Maxi likes the birthday cake, too and eats it with a smile on his face.

Today is Jane's birthday. In the afternoon ten boys and girls come to her house. They all have presents for her. She takes the presents, opens them and says thank you.

In the evening Jane was very happy.
She went to her room and wrote in her diary.*
* *diary* = Tagebuch

Schreibe auf, was Jane in ihr Tagebuch schrieb.
Achtung: Denke daran, dass sie ihr Tagebuch in der Ich-Form und in der Vergangenheit (*simple past*) schreibt.

Friday, 22nd April

Today was my birthday. Ten boys and girls came to my house.

They all

3 A letter from a friend

Das Datum von heute

____

Simple past: questions with and without question words

Lies dir Shanes Brief durch.

Dear Tim, London, 25th August

Thank you for your letter. Now I can answer all your questions. I went to Spain on holiday this summer. No, I didn't go alone. I went with my parents. We stayed there for two weeks. The weather was sunny and warm. Yes, I went swimming every day. No, the water wasn't very cold. Yes, I met a lot of girls. I played volleyball with them. No, I didn't see any sharks*. That's a silly question. There are no sharks in Spain.

I got back to London on 20th August.

Love, Shane

**shark* = Haifisch

Schreibe du jetzt Tims Brief, auf den Shane hier geantwortet hat. Du sollst noch neun Fragen formulieren. Nach den unterstrichenen Angaben in Shanes Brief musst mit dem richtigen Fragewort fragen, z. B. *to Spain* ➜ *Where.*

Dear Shane,

Where did you go on holiday this summer?

____

____

____

Love,

Fragen mit *Who* und *What* können nach einem Subjekt oder einem Objekt fragen. Wenn nach dem Objekt gefragt wird, muss in der Frage do bzw. does (*simple present*) oder did (*simple past*) benutzt werden. Ein Beispiel: *Who did Shane write to?* An wen schrieb Shane? Shane schrieb an Tim. Wenn nach dem Subjekt gefragt wird, wird kein *do*, *does* oder *did* in der Frage benutzt. Ein Beispiel: *Who wrote to Shane?* Wer schrieb Shane? Tim schrieb Shane.

Schreibe zu den folgenden Sätzen jeweils eine Frage nach dem Subjekt und eine Frage nach dem Objekt.

The animals ate the fruits. *Who ate the fruits?*

What did the animals eat?

My father cleaned the table.

The children helped Mr Floyd.

Lorraine caught the ball.

Das Datum von heute ____________

4 On holiday

Simple past in all forms (statements, questions, negative sentences)

Dear Mum,
We are having a lovely time here in Portsmouth. The weather is great and the hotel is OK. But the food isn't very good. We went for a swim before breakfast. Last night Susan and I went to a disco. It was great. I met a nice boy!
Love,
Jane

Mrs Floyd
22 Green Road
Sheffield XCF 123
England

Dear Bernhard,
It's great here in France. It's hot and the water's warm. I spoke French to the waiters in the hotel yesterday. And I watched French TV in the evening.
Yours,
Lorraine

Bernhard Docherty
8 London Road
Edinburgh BYS 129
Scotland

Bilde jetzt Aussagesätze (✔), Negativsätze (✘) oder Fragen(?) mit den angegeben Satzteilen. Bei Fragen bilde dazu die Antworten.

1. Where / Lorraine / to go on holiday (?) *Where did Lorraine go on holiday? Lorraine went to France on holiday.*

2. Jane / to go for a swim / before dinner (✘) ______

3. Jane / to meet / boy / disco (✔) ______

4. Lorraine / to watch / French TV / all day (✘) ______

5. Lorraine / to write to / postcard / her mother (✘) ______

6. Jane / to go / disco / last night (✔) ______

7. Lorraine / to have / good weather (✔) ______

8. Susan / to go / Portsmouth / with Jane (✔) ______

9. Jane / to stay / Where (?) ______

5 A football game

Das Datum von heute ______

Simple present – simple past

Der alte Mr Floyd erinnert sich an den Fußball zu seiner Jugendzeit. Sein Enkel Tom bestätigt, dass es heute genauso ist. Schreibe auf, was Tom sagt.

Mr Floyd: "When I was young the players practised four times a week."

Tom: *"They practise four times a week these days*, too."*

Mr Floyd: "When I was young the referee was fair."

Tom: "______ *these days, too."*

Mr Floyd: "When I was young there were sponsors for each team."

Tom: "______ *these days, too."*

Mr Floyd: "When I was young the fans came to the game every week."

Tom: "______ *these days, too."*

Mr Floyd: "When I was young fair play was very important."

Tom: "______ *these days, too."*

* *these days* = heutzutage

Jetzt erzählt Tom, was heute so alles beim Fußball passiert. Sein Großvater, der alte Mr Floyd, sagt, dass es früher manchmal anders und manchmal ganz genauso war. Schreibe auf, was der Großvater sagt.

1. Tom: "Today lots of fans buy season tickets." • Mr Floyd: *"Oh no: When I was young the fans ______."*

2. Tom: "Today you can buy tea in the stadium." • Mr Floyd: *"Yes, when I was young ______, too."*

3. Tom: "Today there are lots of hooligans." • Mr Floyd: *"No, when I was young ______ not any ______."*

4. Tom: "Today the players don't pay for their football shoes." • Mr Floyd: *"Oh, really?! No, when I was young ______."*

5. Tom: "Today lots of fans watch the game on television."
   • Mr Floyd: *"Yes, when I was young ______, too."*

6. Tom: "Today each team has its own doctor."
   • Mr Floyd: *"Yes, when I was young ______, too."*

7. Tom: "Today the players get a lot of money." • Mr Floyd: *"No, when I was young ______."*

8. Tom: "Today a lot of good players go to Italian football clubs." • Mr Floyd: *"Yes, when I was young ______, too."*

6 Interview with a star

Das Datum von heute

____

Questions and answers in the simple present and simple past

This is an interview with the famous* basketball player Michaela Garden.

Trage die folgenden Formen von *to do* in den Text ein.
Eine Form von *to do* bleibt übrig. Welche ist es? Trage sie hier ein: __________

does – didn't – do – did – do – doesn't – do – didn't – does – did – do – do – doesn't – did – do – does – do – do – does – does – did – don't – doesn't – didn't

Interviewer: "Hello, Mrs Garden. I'd like to ask you some questions. When [1]________ you start playing basketball?" • Michaela: "I started playing basketball fifteen years ago." • I.: "[2]___________ you join a basketball club when you

* *famous* = berühmt

were six?" • M.: "No, I 3 __________. I played in the streets." • "I.: How often 4 ________ you play basketball now?" • M.: "Normally I play five times a week." I.: "5 ________ you have any brothers or sisters?" • M.: "Yes, I 6 __________. I have one brother." • I.: "7 __________ he play basketball, too?" • M.: "No, he 8 __________. He hates it." • I.: "9 __________ your parents like basketball?" • M.: "Yes, they 10 __________." • I.: "11 __________ your father read a lot about basketball?" • M.: "Yes, he 12 __________. He reads a lot, but he 13 ______ watch basketball games on TV." • I.: "14 __________ your father play basketball when he was young?" • M.: "No, he 15 __________. He wasn't tall enough." • I.: "16 _______ you eat anything special before a basketball game?" • M.: "No, I 17 __________. I eat whatever I like." • I.: "When 18 ________ you go to bed?" • M.: "I go to bed at nine o'clock." • I.: " 19 ______ the games start in the morning or in the afternoon?" • M.: "They normally start in the afternoon. "• I.: "20 ________ your parents watch every game you played in last year?" • M.: "No, they 21 __________." • I.: "22 ________ your mother like basketball, too?" • M.: "Yes, she 23 __________." • I.: "Thank your for the interview, Mrs Garden."

Mit dem *simple past* berichtet man über Vergangenes, daher steht es oft zusammen mit Zeitangaben wie diesen: *yesterday, 15 years ago, last week, last year*.
Regelmäßige Verben erhalten im *simple past* die Endung *-ed*: *to live – lived, to start – started*.
Unregelmäßige Verben haben im *simple past* besondere Formen, die du lernen musst, z. B.: *to eat – ate, to come – came, to buy – bought*.

7 Next year

Das Datum von heute

Will-future

Die ganze Familie Floyd denkt über das nächste Jahr nach. Sie haben sehr unterschiedliche Erwartungen, Hoffnungen und auch Befürchtungen. Bilde aus den angegebenen Satzteilen Sätze mit dem *will*-Future.

Das Futur mit *will* wird gebildet aus *will* und dem Infinitv eines Verbs.
Die Kurzform von *will* ist *'ll*.
Das Futur hat für alle Personen die gleiche Form:
We will* (oder: *We'll*) *leave together*: *You will* (oder: *you'll*) *leave tomorrow, he will* (oder: *he'll*) *leave tomorrow and I will* (oder: *I'll*) *leave tomorrow, too.
Das Futur beschreibt zukünftige Ereignisse und drückt Hoffnungen oder Vermutungen über die Zukunft aus.
Sehr oft steht es mit diesen Verben: *to think, to hope, to expect, to promise*.

Mr. Floyd: to buy / next year / a new car

I think I will buy a new car next year.

1. Mrs Floyd: I / to do / next year / more sports *I think*

2. Tom: daddy / to buy / next year / a new car *I hope*

3. Grandpa Floyd: to be / the next year / a cold year. *I think*

4. Jane: my own room / I / to get / next year *I think*

5. Maxi, Jane's dog: to move / next year / to the country / the family

Maybe the family

Einige in der Familie haben gute Vorsätze für das nächste Jahr.
Bilde Sätze mit dem *will*-Futur.

1. Jane: for a walk / the dog / more often (öfter) / to take / next year

I promise I will

2. Mr Floyd: to go shopping / once a week (einmal in der Woche) / next year

I promise

3. Grandpa Floyd: in the living room / to stop / smoking cigars / next year

I promise

8 The weather

Das Datum von heute

Going to-future

London: very overcast with heavy rain = stark bewölkt mit strömendem Regen;
Wales: glorious sunshine = strahlender Sonnenschein;
Scotland: sunny and a bit cloudy = sonnig und leicht bewölkt;
Northern Ireland: cloudy, rain with some sunny spells = bewölkt, Regen mit sonnigen Abschnitten; *the east of England: rainy*

Tom is with his parents in Wales, at the foot of Snowdon*.
He wants to climb Snowdon tomorrow. He phones his friend Shane to find out what the weather will be like.

* *Mount Snowdon is the highest mountain in Wales and England.*

Ergänze die Lücken mit Hilfe der angegebenen Textteile unter dem Bild in dem Gespräch zwischen Shane und Tom.

Tom: "Hi, Shane. Did you see the weather forecast on TV? I want to know what the weather _is going to be_ like on Mount Snowdon." • Shane: "Hi, Tom. Well, in London it's 1 ______________________ _heavy rain_." • Tom: "I don't want to know about London. It _is going to rain_ in North Wales, isn't it?" • Shane: "Wait a minute. In Scotland it 2 ______________________." • Tom: "Not Scotland: what about Mount Snowdon?" • Shane: "In the east of England it's 3 ______________________" • Tom: "No, not England. Listen: I am in North Wales!" • Shane: "Oh, oh. In Northern Ireland it 4 ______________________." • Tom: "Shane! What about Mount Snowdon?" • Shane: "Why do you want to know? What _are you going to do_ there?" • Tom: "I 5 ______________________ Mount Snowdon tomorrow. Now tell me what the weather 6 ______________________ like for Mount Snowdon tomorrow." • Shane: "Have you got a good anorak with you?" • Tom: "Yes, is it going to rain?" • Shane: "No, it 7 ______________________ ______________________. So you can leave your anorak at your hotel!!"

Das Futur mit *going to* besteht aus drei Teilen: *am* / *is* / *are*, *going to* und dem Infinitiv des Verbs:
I am going to do my homework. He is going to climb the mountain.
Das Futur mit *going to* drückt ein Ereignis in der nahen Zukunft, ein Vorhaben aus.

9 Into the future

Das Datum von heute

Going to- and will-future

Das Futur mit *will* drückt oft eher unsichere Vorhersagen (z. B. Wetter) und Vermutungen aus, die man nicht beeinflussen kann.
Oft steht es nach *maybe, I think / I hope / I promise..., I'm sure*.
Das Futur mit *going to* bringt eher ein Vorhaben oder sichere Ankündigungen für die Zukunft zum Ausdruck.

Ergänze die Lücken mit der richtigen Futurform des Verbs in Klammern.

1. I think it 1 _______________ (to be) an interesting game tonight.
2. I'm sure Schalke 2 _______________________ (to win).
3. My Dad 3 _________________________ (to watch) the game with me on TV.
4. My sister 4 ___________________________ (not to watch) the game with us. She hates football.
5. She 5 ________ probably _________ (to tell) us again how stupid football is.
6. I hope one day she 6 ______________________________ (to understand) us.
7. Maybe Daddy 7 ____________________________________ (to tell) her some interesting things about football.
8. It 8 ___________________ (to be) hard, but he 9 ___________________ (to try).
9. Maybe we 10 ______________________________ (to watch) football with the whole family one day!
10. But tonight Mum and my sister 11 _________________ (to go) to the cinema.

Jetzt bastele ein Himmel-und-Hölle-Spiel. Mit Hilfe der Zeichnungen ist das kein Problem für dich. Das fertige Spiel hat acht Innenflächen.
Schreibe auf jede einen der folgenden Sätze. Die vier Sätze, die man jeweils gleichzeitig sehen kann, buchstabierst du von a bis d. Jetzt kannst du deinen Freunden etwas über ihre Zukunft verraten. Du hältst ihnen dein geschlossenes Himmel-und-Hölle-Spiel vor und bittest sie, eine Zahl zwischen 1 und 20 und einen der ersten vier Buchstaben des Alphabets zu nennen (z. B. 7a). Zähle laut die genannte Zahl vor und öffne und schließe dabei dein Himmel-und-Hölle-Spiel. Hast du zu Ende gezählt, liest du den Satz vor, der bei dem genannten Buchstaben steht.

- you are going to have 8 children.
- you are going to marry a millionaire.
- your school is going to close for 10 weeks.
- you are going to live in America.

- your friend ____________________ (Name) is going to become a pop star.
- you are going to win a holiday.
- your brother is going to be on television.
- your parents are going to give you a dog for Christmas.

- je 1x über die Hälfte knicken
- von unten mit Daumen und Zeigefinger in die Täschchen greifen

10 City, town and village

Das Datum von heute

Comparison with -er, -est, good, bad

It's six o'clock in the morning in three very different places. In a big city, a little town and a small village. Let us compare these three places.

	City	Town	Village
	very clean very quiet no traffic	clean quiet some cars	dirty noisy a cock crows, a tractor
Inhabitants	450.000	50.000	250
Bus service to the shopping-centre:	every 10 min.	every 60 min	twice a day

Adjektive kann man steigern.
Einsilbige Adjektive und Adjektive auf -y steigert man, indem man -er und -est anhängt. Ausnahmen: *good – better – best / bad – worse – worst*.

Vergleiche die drei Orte. Sieh dir dazu die Bilder genau an.
Verwende dabei die angegebenen Adjektive.
Schreibe die Sätze auf ein extra Blatt.

1. city – village (clean) *The city is cleaner than the village.*
2. village – town (noisy) *At six a.m. the village is noisier than the town.*
3. city (big) *The city is the biggest place.*
4. the bus service in the town – the bus service in the city (bad)
5. village – city (small)
6. village – town (dirty)
7. town – city (dirty)
8. village – city (busy)
9. city (quiet)
10. the bus service in the town – the bus service in the city (good)
11. town – city (busy)
12. village (dirty)
13. city – village (quiet)
14. village (small)

11 Traffic

Das Datum von heute

Comparisons with more and most

sports car	**family car**	**van**	**truck**
£ 30.500	£ 20.775	£ 23.100	£ 50.000
110 KW	44 KW	50 KW	200 KW

Mr Floyd wants to buy a new car. You can see four different cars here.
He compares the prices and the engines.

Alle Adjektive,
– die drei und mehr Silben haben, oder
– die zwei Silben haben und nicht auf -y enden,
steigert man mit *more* / *most* und *less* / *least*.

***expensive* – teuer *more expensive* – teurer *most expensive* – am teuersten**
***less expensive* – nicht so teuer, billiger *least expensive* – am wenigsten teuer**
***famous* – berühmt *more famous* – berühmter *most famous* – am berühmtesten**
***less famous* – weniger berühmt *least famous* – am wenigsten berühmt**

Vergleiche die Fahrzeuge und benutze dabei die Adjektive *expensive*, *powerful* oder *useful*.

1. a sports car / a family car (expensive)

   The sports car is more expensive than the family car. Oder:

   The familiy car is less expensive than the sports car.

2. the truck / the van (powerful)

   ____

3. the van / the sports car (useful)

   ____

4. the van / the family car (powerful)

____

5. the family car / the sports car (useful)

____

6. the truck (expensive) ______________________________

7. the sports car / the van (expensive) ______________________

____

8. the truck (powerful) ______________________________

Einige Adjektive werden unregelmäßig gesteigert.
Hier zwei wichtige Beispiele:
good **– gut** ***better*** **– besser** ***best*** **– am besten**
bad **– schlecht** ***worse*** **– schlechter** ***worst*** **– am schlechtesten**

Scriptor macht sich auch so seine Gedanken zu dem neuen Auto.
Schreibe auf, was Scriptor über die vier unterschiedlichen Autos denkt.

1. the sports car (small) ______________________________

2. the family car / the sports car (comfortable)

____

3. the sports car (dangerous) ___________________________

4. the truck / the van (bad) ______________________ *for a family.*

5. the family car / the sports car / (useful) ___________________

______________________________________ *for a family.*

6. the familiy car (good) / for me ______________________

12 Grammar darts

Das Datum von heute

____

Mixed comparisons

Im inneren Kreis der Dartscheibe stehen sechs Adjektive. Trage die fehlenden Steigerungsformen in den mittleren und äußeren Kreis der Dartscheibe ein.

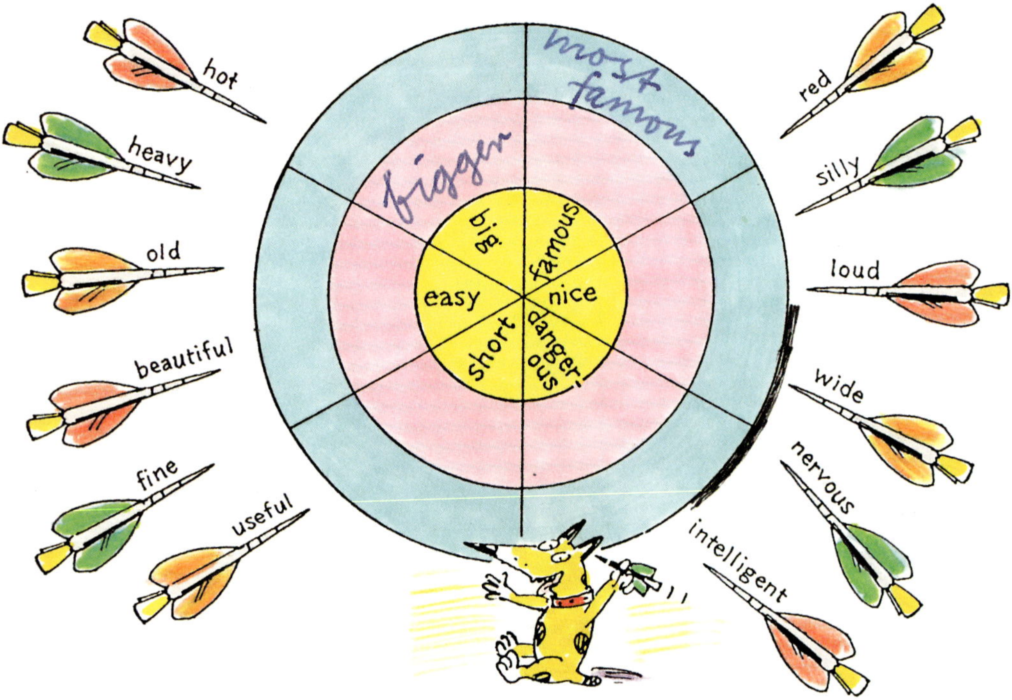

Jetzt kannst du bestimmt die Adjektive an den Dartpfeilen und die Adjektive auf der Scheibe zuordnen. Welche bilden ihre Steigerung auf die gleiche Weise? Trage sie hier ein:

easy / easier – heavy / heavier • big / bigger – hot / ...

____

____

Lorraine und Tim gehen zum ersten Mal in ein Sportzentrum. Auf der Preisliste sehen sie, was eine Trainerstunde in verschiedenen Sportarten kostet. Für schwierigere Sportarten muss man mehr Stunden nehmen als für leichtere. Sie vergleichen die Sportarten. Schreibe die Sätze ihres Gesprächs auf.

	price for one lesson	**number of lessons**
tennis	£ 15	15 lessons
badminton	£ 11	12 lessons
squash	£ 12	10 lessons
table tennis	£ 10	8 lessons

Tim: tennis / squash: difficult *"Tennis is more difficult than squash."*

Lorraine: tennis: expensive *"Tennis is the most expensive sport here."*

Lorraine: table tennis / badminton: easy

1. ______________________________

Tim: squash / badminton: expensive

2. ______________________________

Tim: table tennis: cheap

3. ______________________________

Lorraine: badminton / table tennis: difficult

4. ______________________________

13 shopping

Das Datum von heute

____

Some – any

Mr Floyd and Jane have to do the shopping today.

Nachdem du dir die folgende Regel durchgelesen hast, trage in die Lücken entweder *some* oder *any* ein.

Reden wir von unbestimmten Mengen, wird in bejahten Aussagesätzen *some* benutzt: *We have some apples*. *Any* wird in verneinten Aussagen und Fragen benutzt: *Do we have any apples*? *No, we don't have any*.

Mr Floyd: "Have we got 1 ________ cornflakes left?" • Jane: "No, we haven't got 2 ________. We have to buy 3 ________." • Mr Floyd: "What about coffee?" • Jane: "That's OK. We don't need 4 ________. There's 5 ________ here. "• Mr Floyd: "I don't think we've got 6 ________ biscuits left. I couldn't find 7 ________ yesterday." • Jane: "Wait a minute. There are 8 ________ under the coffee." • Mr Floyd: "Do we need 9 ________ jam?" • Jane: "Yes, we need 10 ________. There isn't 11 ________ left." • Mr Floyd: "Fine. Let's get 12 ________ strawberry jam this week. And I think we need 13 ________ bread." • Jane: "Yes there isn't 14 ________. You ate the last piece this morning."

Tom doesn't like supermarkets so he always goes to Mrs Martin's shop. But Mrs Martin doesn't always have everything he needs.

In der Tabelle siehst du einige Dinge, die Mrs Martin heute da hat und einige, die sie nicht da hat. Ergänze das Gespräch zwischen ihr und Tom. Benutze die Angaben in Klammern und *some* oder *any*.

Yes, I've got ...	No, I haven't got ...
cornflakes, coffee, strawberry jam, bread	tomatoes, French cheese, peanut butter

Tom: "Hi Mrs Martin." • Mrs Martin: "Hello Tom. What can I do for you?"

1. Tom: "We need ________ cornflakes. Have you got ________?"
2. Mrs Martin: "Yes, I've got ________. Here they are."
3. Tom: (French cheese) "OK. Have you got ______________________________?"
4. Mrs Martin: "I'm sorry. /______________________________."
5. Tom: (coffee, peanut butter) Have______________________________

____

6. Mrs Martin: ____

____

7. Tom: (jam, bread): ____
8. Mrs Martin: ____.
9. Tom: "I forgot my money! I haven't got ________ money at all! I'll run home and get________! Sorry, Mrs Martin!"

14 Oh Maxi!

Das Datum von heute

____

Some – any and their compounds

Maxi ran away. Now Jane's dog is back home ...

Überlege, welches Wort aus der Liste du für die Lücken nehmen musst. Streiche die Worte durch, die du verwendet hast. Du musst alle Worte verwenden. Du findest auf der nächsten Seite eine Regel zur Verwendung dieser Worte.

anyone – someone – something – anything – something – anything – somewhere – anything – someone – someone – anything

Mrs Floyd: "You stupid dog! You don't understand 1 ______________, do you? When 2 ______________ calls you: you don't come. When 3 ______________ wants to play with you: you walk away. And now all this dirt! Is there 4 ______________ still clean in this room? I think you spent the afternoon 5 ______________ in the forest. Did you find 6 ______________ interesting?

LÖSUNGEN

1

☆ Spaceshuttle; Crew; Check; Airbag; Receiver; Handy; bootet bzw. booten; Computer; E-mail; Aliens; groggy; Take-off; Mountainbikes; Jogging; Bodybuilding; fit; Kids; Moonboots; Kingsize; Overalls; cool.

☆☆ Bei einigen Wörtern findest du in deinem *dictionary* viele mögliche Bedeutungen. Wir haben hier nur die Übersetzung aufgeschrieben, die für unseren Text wichtig oder interessant sind.

1. Airbag = Luftsack;
2. Alien = außerirdisches Wesen;
3. Bodybuilding = (Körper + Bauen =) Krafttraining;
4. booten = (das Betriebssystem des Computers) laden; ursprünglich kommt es von boot – Stiefel und heißt: gestiefelt, fertig loszugehen;
5. Check = Überprüfung;
6. Computer = Rechner;
7. cool = klasse;
8. Crew = Besatzung, Mannschaft;
9. E-mail = elektronische Post;
10. fit = gesund, in Form;
11. groggy = benommen, angeschlagen;
12. Handy = (Adjektiv) praktisch, griffbereit;
13. Jogging = Dauerlauf machen;
14. Kids = Kinder, Jugendliche;
15. Kingsize = (König + Größe =) besonders groß;
16. Moonboot = (Mond + Stiefel =) gemeint sind Stiefel, die so aussehen, wie die Stiefel von Astronauten;
17. Mountainbike = Bergfahrrad;
18. Overall = Arbeitsanzug;
19. Receiver = Empfänger;
20. Spaceshuttle = (Weltraum + etwas, das hin- und herpendelt – z. B. shuttle-bus = ein Bus, der zwischen zwei Orten hin- und herpendelt =) Raumfähre;
21. Take-off = Start, Abflug.

2

☆
1. Today is Jane's birthday ...;
2. They play games ...;
3. Then Jane's mother turns on the light again ...;
4. Tom has something in his hand ...;
5. At eight o'clock the party ...

Today was my birthday. Ten boys and girls came to my house. They all had presents for me. I took the presents, opened them and said thank-you. We played games. In one game Tom turned off the light and tried to catch the other children. Suddenly he fell over something. He lay on the floor. He couldn't get up. My mother turned on the light again. We couldn't see Tom. Where was he? Then I saw Tom under the table with Maxi, my dog. Tom had something in his hand. It was a piece of cake. But Maxi liked the birthday cake, too and ate it with a smile on his face. At eight o'clock the party was over. The children went home and I went to my room.

3

Did you go alone? How long did you stay? What was the weather like? Did you go swimming every day? Was the water very cold? Did you meet a lot of girls? What did you play with them? Did you see any sharks? When did you get back to London?

Who cleaned the table? What did my father clean? / Who helped Mr Floyd? Who did the children help? / Who caught the ball? What did Lorraine catch?

4

2. Jane didn't go for a swim before dinner.
3. Jane met a boy at the disco.
4. Lorraine didn't watch French TV all day.
5. Lorraine didn't write a postcard to her mother.
6. Jane went to the disco last night.
7. Lorraine had good weather.
8. Susan went to Portsmouth with Jane.
9. Where did Jane stay? She stayed in a hotel.

5

The referee is fair these days, too. – There are sponsors for each team these days, too. – The fans come to the game every week these days, too. – Fair play is very important these days, too.

1. Oh no: When I was young the fans didn't buy season tickets.
2. Yes, when I was young you could buy tea in the stadium, too.
3. No, when I was young there were not (weren't) any hooligans.
4. Oh, really?! No, when I was young the players paid for their football shoes.
5. Yes, when I was young lots of fans watched the game on television, too.
6. Yes, when I was young each team had its own doctor, too.
7. No, when I was young players didn't get a lot of money.
8. Yes, when I was young a lot of good players went to Italian football clubs, too.

6

1 did; **2** Did; **3** didn't; **4** do; **5** Do; **6** do; **7** Does; **8** doesn't; **9** Do; **10** do; **11** Does; **12** does; **13** doesn't; **14** Did; **15** didn't; **16** Do; **17** don't; **18** do; **19** Do; **20** Did; **21** didn't; **22** Does; **23** does – Doesn't bleibt übrig.

7

☆ 1. I think I will do more sports next year.
2. I hope daddy will buy a new car next year.
3. I think the next year will be a cold year.
4. I think I will get my own room next year.
5. Maybe the family will move to the country next year.

☆☆ 1. I promise I will take the dog for a walk more often next year.
2. I promise I will go shopping once a week next year.
3. I promise I will stop smoking cigars in the living room next year.

8

☆ 1. going to be very overcast with heavy rain;
2. is going to be sunny and a bit cloudy;
3. going to be rainy ODER going to rain;
4. is going to be cloudy and rainy with some sunny spells ODER is going to rain a little bit;
5. am going to climb;
6. is going to be;
7. isn't going to rain.

9

☆ 1. will be;
2. will win;
3. is going to watch;
4. is not going to watch;
5. will probably tell;
6. will understand;
7. will tell;
8. will be;
9. is going to try
10. will watch;
11. are going to go.

10

☆ 4. The bus service in the town is worse than the bus service in the city.
5. The village is smaller than the city.
6. The village is dirtier than the town.
7. The town is dirtier than the city.
8. The village is busier than the city.
9. The city is the quietest place.
10. The bus service in the city is better than the bus service in the town.
11. The town is busier than the city.
12. The village is the dirtiest place.
13. The city is quieter than the village.
14. The village is the smallest place.

11

☆ 2. The truck is more powerful than the van. The van is less powerful than the truck.
3. The van is more useful than the sports car. The sports car is less useful than the van.
4. The van is more powerful than the family car. The family car is less powerful than the van.
5. The family car is more useful than the sports car. The sports car is less useful than the family car.
6. The truck is the most expensive (car).
7. The sports car is more expensive than the van. The van is less expensive than the sports car.
8. The truck is the most powerful (car).

☆☆ 1. The sports car is the smallest.
2. The family car is more comfortable than the sports car. The sports car is less comfortable than the family car.
3. The sports car is the most dangerous.
4. The truck is worse than the van for a family. The van is better than the truck for a family.
5. The family car is more useful than the sports car for a family. The sports car is less useful than the family car for a family.
6. The family car is the best for me.

12

☆

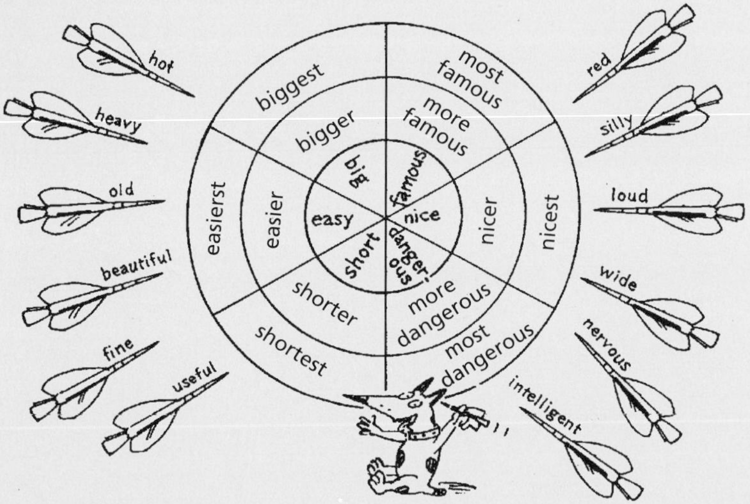

☆☆ big / bigger; hot / hotter; red / redder • famous / more famous; nervous / more nervous; useful / more useful • nice / nicer; wide / wider; fine / finer • dangerous / more dangerous; intelligent / more intelligent; beautiful / more beautiful • short / shorter; loud / louder; old / older • easy / easier; heavy / heavier; silly / sillier •

☆☆
1. Table tennis is easier than badminton.
2. Squash is more expensive than badminton.
3. Table tennis is the cheapest sport here.
4. Badminton is more difficult than table tennis.

13

☆ **1.** any; **2.** any; **3.** some; **4.** any; **5.** some; **6.** any; **7.** any; **8.** some; **9.** any; **10.** some; **11.** any; **12.** some; **13.** some; **14.** any.

☆☆
1. some; any
2. some;
3. any French cheese;
4. I haven't got any French cheese;
5. Have you got any coffee and any peanut butter?
6. I've (I have) got some coffee but I haven't got any peanut butter.
7. Have you got any jam and any bread?
8. Yes, I've (I have) got some jam and some bread;
9. any; some.

14

☆ **1.** anything; **2.** someone; **3.** someone; **4.** anything; **5.** somewhere; **6.** anything; **7.** something; **8.** anything; **9.** something; **10.** someone; **11.** anyone.

☆☆ **1.** something; **2.** anything; **3.** something, **4.** anywhere; **5.** anything; **6.** anything; **7.** anything; **8.** some; **9.** anybody; **10.** somebody.

15

☆ **1.** mustn't; **2.** needn't; **3.** can; **4.** mustn't; **5.** needn't = Er kann eine Woche zu Hause bleiben. (auch mustn't ist möglich: Er darf eine Woche nicht in die Schule gehen.); **6.** needn't; **7.** must; **8.** needn't; **9.** must; **10.** mustn't; **11.** needn't; **12.** must.

☆☆ **1.** mustn't drive faster than 50 mph; **2.** mustn't; **3.** must; **4.** needn't; **5.** must; **6.** needn't; **7.** mustn't; **8.** must.

16

☆ brother; bus; car; church; classroom; daughter.

☆☆ *Die Verbformen des Textes sind*: is, goes, doesn't go, goes, takes, runs, comes, plays, doesn't read, watches.
Der Text im simple past: Last Monday the weather was fine and Jane went to town. She didn't go by bus. She went by bike. Jane took her dog Maxi with her. Maxi ran very fast. When Jane came home, she played basketball with her friends. In the evening she didn't read a book, she watched TV.

a) Where does Mr Brown work on Saturday afternoons?
b) What did she buy?
c) When do the Millers always get up?
d) Where do the children never play football?

a) will; **b)** is going to; **c)** are going to; **d)** is going to.

a) A motorbike is more dangerous than a car.
b) A van is heavier than a motorbike.
c) A motorbike is faster than a car.
d) A sports car is more interesting than a truck.

a) any; **b)** some; **c)** any; **d)** anything; **e)** something.

17

A – J; B – E; C – L; D – H; G – K; I – F; M – N

18

2. Jane has already put the dishes on the shelf.
3. Tom has just put the milk into the fridge.
4. They've just cleaned the floor.
5. Jane has already taken out the rubbish.
6. Jane and Tom have just made a cake.
7. Jane has just watered the plants.
8. They've already gone shopping.

19

2. I haven't learned any history yet.
3. I haven't finished the picture yet.
4. I haven't bought a new exercise book yet.
5. I haven't drawn a map of Great Britain yet.
6. I haven't collected any flowers yet.
7. I haven't learned my English vocabulary yet.
8. I haven't repaired my school bag yet.
9. I haven't written a story yet.
10. I haven't written a German essay yet.
11. I haven't made a survey about the traffic in our town yet.
12. I haven't read the end of the book about Robin Hood yet.

1. She hasn't done her maths homework yet. **5.** She hasn't drawn a map of Great Britain yet. **9.** She hasn't written a story yet. **12.** She hasn't read the end of the book about Robin Hood yet.

20

1. Have you ever had a pet? **2.** Have you always kept your dogs in the house? **3.** Have you ever sold one of your dogs? **4.** Have you always given your dog proper food?

5. Why have you decided to buy another dog? **6.** Why have you come to me?

☆☆ **1.** Where have you put the dog? I have put the dog in the bird cage.
2. What has happened to the bird? Nothing has happened to the bird.

21

☆ **1.** booked; **2.** picked up; **3.** haven't got; **4.** Have you decided; **5.** talked; **6.** Did you phone; **7.** called; **8.** hasn't come; **9.** checked; **10.** has come; **11.** has just brought; **12.** haven't asked; **13.** checked; **14.** were; **15.** haven't looked.

☆☆ I met Peter two years ago. **2.** He has been a good friend ever since. **3.** I met him last Saturday. 4. He hasn't phoned me yet.

22

☆ **1.** will I get; **2.** needed; **3.** bought; **4.** need; **5.** buys; **6.** will get; **7.** will buy; **8.** will get; **9.** will buy.

☆☆ **1.** help; **2.** need; **3.** haven't decided; **4.** do you take; **5.** take; **6.** Have you ever had; **7.** haven't; **8.** got; **9.** are; **10.** will go; **11.** don't like; **12.** bought; **13.** am; **14.** haven't got; **15.** sold; **16.** will get; **17.** will come.

23

☆ Did you ride very fast on your mountain bike? – Did the boy on the skateboard cross the street? – Have you been in the same class for a long time? – Are you friends? – Where did the ambulance take you? – Has he ever had an accident before? – Will you go to school tomorrow?

24

☆☆ **1.** The cinema is next to the school (on the right).
2. The museum is behind the church. ODER The museum is opposite the church.
3. The pet shop is opposite the cinema.
4. The book shop is between the butcher's shop and the post office.
5. In front of the café are tables and chairs.
6. The library is behind the supermarket.
7. The bank-robber is in front of the bank.
8. The museum is next to the toy shop (on the left).

25

☆ **1.** at; **2.** on; **3.** On; **4.** in; **5.** at; **6.** in; **7.** On; **8.** before; **9.** after; **10.** on; **11.** At; **12.** past; **13.** on; **14.** after; **15.** on; **16.** from; **17.** till; **18.** On; **19.** from; **20.** till; **21.** At; **22.** in; **23.** on; **24.** in; **25.** after. – Wenn du alle Lücken richtig ausgefüllt hast, muss am Ende einmal „at" übrig bleiben.

26

☆ **2.** You should send your letters at the beginning of December.
3. You should write the address on the front of the envelope.
4. Don't forget to put the stamp in the right corner.
5. Do you want to send it by airmail?
6. Put an airmail sticker on the envelope then.

☆☆ **1.** How much is a postcard to Germany?
2. I need ten stamps for postcards to Germany. And I need one stamp for a postcard to the USA.
3. Yes, I'd like to send it by airmail. Have you got any nice stamps?
4. Can you put on the airmail sticker for me, please?
5. Thank you very much.

27

☆ slowly **(M)** noisy **(O)** well **(T)** carefully **(O)** quickly **(R)** dangerous **(B)** easily **(I)** bad **(K)** nervously **(E)** unhappy **(S)** – Ann is interested in motorbikes.

☆☆ **1.** well; **2.** wonderful; **3.** wonderfully; **4.** hungry.

28

☆ **a)** Peter has just done his homework.
b) Have the boys gone shopping yet?
c) The girls haven't won a hockey game this year.
d) Has your teacher given back the English test?
e) My friend and I have been in town.
f) John hasn't bought a new exercise book yet.

☆☆ **1.** saw; **2.** haven't seen; **3.** thought; **4.** asked; **5.** didn't know; **6.** called; **7.** came; **8.** have you seen; **9.** asked; **10.** said; **11.** stole; **12.** reported.

☆☆☆ Die richtigen Zeitformen sind: **a)** will rain; **b)** bought; **c)** haven't done; **d)** played.

☆☆☆☆ **1.** in; **2.** at; **3.** in; **4.** in.

☆☆☆☆☆ Die richtigen Formen sind: **a)** carefully; **b)** slowly; **c)** angry; **d)** She plays well. / She is a good player.

29

☆ Die geheime Nachricht lautet: NOW YOU KNOW A LOT OF ENGLISH! WELL DONE.

☆☆ Die 17 gesuchten Wörter ergeben einen guten Tipp, wie du überall englische Vokabeln lernen kannst:
WRITE YOUR WORDS ON CARDS, ONE SIDE ENGLISH THE OTHER SIDE GERMAN. THEN YOU CAN LEARN EVERYWHERE.

I'm sure you found 7 ____________ interesting. But I don't want to know. The best thing is I don't know 8 ________________. One day 9 ______________ will happen to you, Maxi. I hope 10 ________________ will be there to help you. What will happen when there isn't 11 _____________ to help you, Maxi?"

Die wichtigsten Zusammensetzungen (*compounds*) von *some* und *any* sind für Personen someone und anyone, für Gegenstände *something* und *anything*, für Orte *somewhere* und *anywhere*. Für sie gelten dieselben Regeln wie für *some* und *any*: *Someone, something* und *somewhere* wird in bejahten Aussagesätzen benutzt. *Anyone, anything* und *anywhere* benutzt man in verneinten Aussagesätzen und in Fragen.

Lies dir den Text durch und trage *some*, *any* oder ein *compound* ein.
Du musst alle angegebenen Worte verwenden.

something – some – something – somebody – anything – anybody – anywhere – anything – anything – anything

Doctor: "Good morning. What's the matter?" • Allen: "There's 1 _____________ wrong with my arm." • Doctor: "Did 2 ______________ serious happen?" • Allen: "No, I fell over 3 ______________ ."• Doctor: "And why?" • Allen: "Because I can't find my glasses 4 _______________. And without my glasses I can't see 5 ______________." • Doctor: "Do you have 6 ______________ to put on your arm?" • Allen: "No, I haven't got 7 ______________ to put on it. Have you got medicine for me?" • Doctor: "Yes, here's 8 ______________ cream. Put it on your arm three times a day. Is there 9 ______________ here to take you home?" • Allen: "No, but I just have to phone home and 10 __________ can come for me."

15 An accident

Das Datum von heute ____________

Modal auxiliaries

Shane ist im Bett. Er hatte gestern einen Unfall.
Sage, was er machen oder nicht machen muss, kann, soll oder darf.

Wir benutzen ein modales Hilfsverb zusammen mit einem Vollverb, um zu sagen, was getan werden muss, kann, darf oder soll: *You can take the book*.
Einige haben eine besondere Bedeutung. Dies sind die wichtigsten:
***Mustn't* drückt ein Verbot aus:**
***You mustn' t eat here*. Du darfst hier nicht essen**
***Needn't* drückt die Wahlmöglichkeit aus:**
***You needn't eat this*. Du musst das nicht essen.**
***Must* benutzt man für 'müssen' an Stelle von *have to*, um einen Zwang oder einen Auftrag auszudrücken: *You must do this*. Du musst das tun!**

He 1 ________ get up but he 2 ________ sleep all day. He 3 ________ watch TV but he 4 ________ get too tired. He 5 ________ go to school for a week. He 6 ________ do any homework but he 7 ________ learn his English vocabulary because he has a test on Monday. He 8 ________ go back to the doctor until next week but he 9 ________ put some cream on his arm three times a day. He hurt his arm and his head so he 10 ________ move his head too much. He 11 ________ have a special diet* but he 12 ________ drink a lot.

* *a special diet* = eine besondere Auswahl von Lebensmitteln

Noch ein Unfall!
Ein *police officer* redet mit einem jungen, unerfahrenen Fahrer.

Setze *needn't*, *must* or *mustn't* ein. Unten findest du einige Vokabelhilfen.

Police officer: "Look at that sign! What does it mean?" 

Learner driver: "You 1 ______ drive faster than ______."

Police officer: "And this sign?" 

Learner driver: "That means that there are traffic lights."

Police officer: "When there is a red light you 2 ______ drive on. You 3 ______ stop. You 4 ______ stop at a zebra crossing, only when somebody wants to cross the road, then you 5 ______ stop. You 6 ______ switch your headlights* on in broad daylight** but you can, if you want. Good. And this sign?"  Learner driver: "You 7 ______ turn left. You 8 ______ turn right or go straight on."

don't drive faster than 50 mph – fahre nicht schneller als 50 (Meilen/Stunde) /
turn right or go straight on – rechts abbiegen oder geradeaus fahren /
always stop at a red light – bleib immer an der roten Ampel stehen /
turn left – links abbiegen

16 Test: Language school

Das Datum von heute ....

Before you can enter the language school*, you must do the following test.
* *language school* = Sprachschule

Bringe die Wörter in die richtige alphabetische Reihenfolge.
a) daughter – brother – bus – church – classroom – car

You get 3 points for the correct alphabetical order. "I have ____ points."

Unterstreiche in dem Text die Verben und schreibe den ganzen Text dann auf einem Blatt Papier im *simple past* auf.
Beginne so: "Last Monday the weather was fine and ..." (Doppelseite 4)
Every Monday when the weather is fine Jane goes to town. She doesn't go by bus, she goes by bike. Jane takes her dog Maxi with her. Maxi runs very fast. When Jane comes home, she plays basketball with her friends. In the evening she doesn't read a book, she watches TV.

You get 1 point for each correct past tense verb form. "I have ____ points."

Schreibe auf ein Blatt die Frage nach dem unterstrichenen Satzteil in der richtigen Zeit. Benutze die Fragewörter *where*, *when* und *what*. (Doppelseite 1)
a) Mr Brown works <u>in the garden</u> on Saturday afternoons.
b) She bought <u>a packet of biscuits</u>.
c) The Millers always get up <u>at seven o'clock</u>.
d) The children never play football <u>in the street</u>.

For each correct question you get 2 points. "I have _____ points."

Setze in die Sätze *will* oder die richtige Form von *going to* ein.
(Doppelseiten 7, 8, 9)

a) I think he ________________ be 13 next year. **b)** Hurry up! The film _____________ start in a few seconds! **c)** They _____________ play football after school. **d)** It ____________ rain. Look at the clouds.

For each correct sentence you get 2 points. "I have ______ points."

Vergleiche folgende Dinge und übersetze die Sätze. (Doppelseiten 10, 11, 12)

a) Ein Motorrad ist gefährlicher als ein Auto.
b) Ein Lieferwagen ist schwerer als ein Motorrad.
c) Ein Motorrad ist schneller als ein Auto.
d) Ein Sportwagen ist interessanter als ein LKW.

For each correct sentence you get 3 points. "I have _____ points."

Setze *some*, *any*, *something* oder *anything* ein. (Doppelseiten 13, 14)

a) Have you got ___________ apples?

b) I need _____________ apples.

c) I'm sorry, but today I haven't got ____________ apples.

d) Is there ________________ else I can do for you?

e) Yesterday I bought ________________ nice for your birthday.

For each correct sentence you get 1 point. "I have ______ points." Now add up all your points. " Out of 47 possible points I have altogether ______ points.
Mehr als 37 Punkte? Sehr gut! Herzlichen Glückwunsch! Ein tolles Ergebnis.
Mehr als 30 Punkte? Gut. Die meisten Schwierigkeiten hast du sicher im Griff.
Weniger als 30 Punkte? Du kannst ganz sicher noch ein besseres Ergebnis erreichen! Welche Doppelseiten fandest du besonders schwierig? Blättere noch einmal durch die ersten 15 Doppelseiten. Schau dir alle Doppelseiten, auf denen du unsicher bist, noch einmal in Ruhe mit dem Lösungsheft an und du wirst ***jeden Tag ein bisschen besser***.
Weniger als 20 Punkte? Dir machen noch zu viele Dinge Schwierigkeiten. Arbeite noch einmal die Doppelseiten 1 — 15 in Ruhe und mit dem Lösungsheft durch. Sicher kann dir auch dein Schulbuch bei deinen Problemen weiterhelfen!

17 Take a break

Das Datum von heute ____________

School jokes

The teacher asks his pupils on a school trip:
"What do you think?
How many sheep are on this farm?"
John: "280 sheep."
Teacher: "How did you find out?"
John: "That was easy. I counted the legs and then divided them by four."

"Today I was the best in class", Tina tells her mother.
"Great", her mother says, "what did you do?"
"The teacher wanted to know 'how much is 6 x 7', and I said '41'."
"But that's wrong, Tina."
"Yes, but I was closest."

Teacher: "I've got ten oranges in one hand and twelve oranges in my other hand. What have I got?"
Pupil: "Big hands."

The teacher asks Susan: "You've got 30 peanuts, half of the peanuts is for your little sister. How many peanuts does your little sister get?"
Susan: "Six."
Teacher: "But that's wrong. Can't you divide 30 by 2?"
Susan: "Of course, I can. But my little sister can't."

Teacher: "Fred, all your homework is wrong again. Haven't you got a brother who can help you?"
Fred: "Not yet, but I'll get one soon."

Hier stehen einige englische Sprichwörter (*proverbs*) und bekannte Aussprüche. Es gibt auch im Deutschen Sprichwörter, die dasselbe bedeuten. Welche deutschen und englischen Sätze passen wohl zusammen? Verbinde sie mit Linien.

A If anything can go wrong, it will. (commonly known as *Murphy's Law*)

F Glück im Spiel, Pech in der Liebe.

K One hand washes the other.

D Out of sight, out of mind.

J Was schief gehen kann, geht schief. (bekannt als *Murphys Law*)

E Knowledge is power.

N Wer zuletzt lacht, lacht am besten.

H Aus dem Auge, aus dem Sinn.

C To err is human.

I Lucky in cards, unlucky in love.

L Irren ist menschlich.

M He who laughs last laughs best.

G Eine Hand wäscht die andere.

B Wissen ist Macht.

18 Jobs in the house

Das Datum von heute

Present perfect statements

Mr und Mrs Floyd waren über das Wochenende weg. Jane und Tom haben den ganzen Nachmittag aufgeräumt, bevor die Eltern zurückkommen. Schau dir die zwei Bilder an, und beschreibe mit den angegebenen Satzteilen was Tom und Jane gemacht haben.

Das *present perfect* wird gebildet aus *have/has* und der 3. Form des Verbs (Partizip Perfekt). Die 3. Form eines Verbs hat bei regelmäßigen Verben dieselbe Form wie das *simple past*.
She has seen the film already. They've just gone.
Wir benutzen das *present perfect* zum Beispiel für Handlungen,
- **die in der Vergangenheit stattgefunden haben, aber ein Ergebnis in der Gegenwart haben,**
- **die in der Vergangenheit begonnen haben und immer noch andauern.**

1. Tom and Jane / the dishes / to wash / just

   Tom and Jane have just washed the dishes.

2. Jane / on the shelf / to put / the dishes / already

   ____

3. the milk / Tom / to put / into the fridge / just

   ____

4. they / the floor / to clean / just

   ____

5. Jane / to take out / the rubbish / already

   ____

6. a cake / Jane and Tom / to make / just

   ____

7. to water / the plants / Jane / just

   ____

8. they / to go shopping / already

   ____

19 My homework

Das Datum von heute

Present perfect negative statements

It's 3 o'clock p. m., a sunny Monday afternoon.
Here's Susan's homework list for this week.

This week's homework:

1. do maths homework
2. learn some history
3. finish the picture
4. buy a new exercise book
5. draw a map of Great Britain
6. collect some flowers
7. learn my English vocabulary
8. repair my school bag
9. write a story
10. write a German essay
11. make a survey* about the traffic in our town
12. read the end of the book about Robin Hood

* *survey* = Untersuchung, Umfrage

Die Verneinung des *present perfect* ist ganz einfach: Hinter *have* bzw. *has* kommt einfach ein *not*.
Bei „noch-nicht-Sätzen" steht im Englischen meist *yet* am Ende des Satzes.
He has not closed the window. I haven't seen this film yet.
(Ich habe diesen Film noch nicht gesehen.)

On her way home from school Susan met her friend Lorraine.
The two girls went to a cafeteria and had a lemonade.
Now it's 5 o'clock p. m. Look at Susan's homework list.

Schreibe auf, was Susan alles noch nicht getan hat.

1. *I haven't done my maths homework yet.*

2. ______

3. ______

4. ______

5. ______

6. ______

7. ______

8. ______

9. ______

10. ______

11. ______

12. ______

Schreibe zu den Sätzen 1., 5., 9. und 12., was Lorraine über Susan sagt:

1. *She* ______ *her* ______

5. ______ *Great Britain yet.*

9. ______

12. ______

20 Keeping a pet

Das Datum von heute

____

Present perfect questions

Jane möchte gerne einen zweiten Hund zu Hause haben, damit Maxi nicht so alleine ist. Aber der Hundezüchter (*the dog breeder*) verkauft nicht jedem einen Hund. Erst vergewissert er sich, dass der Kunde etwas von Tieren versteht.

Ergänze die Fragen, indem du die Verben im *present perfect* schreibst.

Im *present perfect* muss nur *have / has* vor das Subjekt an den Anfang des Satzes gestellt werden, um eine Frage zu bilden:
***Has she gone home already*? Ist sie schon nach Hause gegangen?**

1. Dog breeder: "________ you ever ________ a pet?" (to have) • Jane: "Yes, we have always had several dogs at home." • **2.** Dog breeder: "__________ you always ________________ your dogs in the house?" (to keep) • Jane: "Yes, we have." • **3.** Dog breeder: "__________ you ever ___________ one of your dogs?" (to sell) • Jane: "No, of course not." • **4.** Dog breeder: "______ you always ______________ your dog proper food?" (to give) • Jane: "Yes, we have always given our dogs good dog-food." • **5.** Dog breeder: "Why ______ you ______________________ to buy another dog?" (to decide) • Jane: "Because our dog Maxi needs a friend to play with." • **6.** Dog breeder: "Why ______ you __________ to me?" (to come) • Jane: "Because I have heard that you're a good breeder but you ask a lot of questions, don't you?"

Klasse! Der Lehrling ist allein in der Tierhandlung. Der Besitzer ruft an, um sich zu vergewissern, ob alles in Ordnung ist.

Schau dir das Bild an und schreibe die Fragen des Besitzers der Tierhandlung und die Antworten des Lehrlings im *present perfect* auf. Benutze die angegebenen Satzteile.

Ein Beispiel:
Pet shop owner: What / to do / with the two white mice?

What have you done with the two white mice?

Assistant: to take / it / home *I have taken it home.*

1. Pet shop owner: Where / to put / the dog?

____

Assistant: to put / the dog / in the birdcage

____

2. Pet shop owner: What / to happen / to the bird?

____

Assistant: Nothing / to happen / to the bird

____

21 At the bank

Das Datum von heute

____

Present perfect – simple past

**Das *present perfect* steht sehr oft in Sätzen, die folgende Zeitangaben enthalten: *already, not yet, ever / never, until now* und *just*.
Eine Handlung hat in der Vergangenheit begonnen, dauert aber vielleicht bis jetzt noch an oder hat jetzt ein Ergebnis.
Das *simple past* finden wir häufig bei diesen Zeitangaben: *yesterday, two days / weeks / months / years ago, last Monday / year* ...
Eine Handlung ist in der Vergangenheit, zu einem bestimmten Zeitpunkt abgeschlossen worden.**

Jetzt kannst du sicher entscheiden, ob in den folgenden Sätzen das Verb im *present perfect* oder *simple past* geschrieben werden muss.

Mrs Floyd and her husband are in the bank. They are talking to the bank manager. • Bank manager: "Good morning. Can I help you?" • Mrs Floyd: "Yes, we 1 ____________ (to book) a holiday in Canada three months ago and 2 ______________ (pick up) the tickets from the travel agent four weeks later. But we 3 __________________ (to have not got) any Canadian money yet." Bank manager: "4 ___________ you 4 __________________ (to decide) how much you need?" • Mrs Floyd: "We 5 _________________ (to talk) about that yesterday and we need 5,000 Canadian dollars." • Bank manager:" 6 ___________ you 6 ________________ (to phone) us yesterday? • Mr Floyd: "Yes, we 7 ___________

(to call) in the afternoon." Bank manager: "The money 8 ______________ (not to come) from the main bank yet." • Mrs Floyd: "That's not good." • Bank manager: "Wait a minute. I 9 ______________ (to check) an hour ago but perhaps it 10 ______________ (to come) since then." • Bank manager: "A man 11 __________ just 11 ______________ (to bring) the money from the main bank. It is here." • Mr Floyd: "We 12 ______________ (not to ask) yet how much a Canadian dollar is." • Bank manager: "I 13 ______________ (to check) yesterday and 5,000 dollars 14 __________ (to be) 750 pounds. But I 15 ______________ (not to look) today yet. But I think it's the same."

Mr Floyd:"That's OK. Thank you."

Bilde ganze Sätze aus den angegebenen Satzteilen und benutze das *present perfect* oder *simple past*.

1. I / to meet / Peter / two years ago.

____

2. He / to be / a good friend / ever since.

____

3. I / to meet / him / last Saturday

____

4. He / not to phone / me / yet

____

22 In a clothes shop

Das Datum von heute

____

Mixed tenses

It's Lorraine's birthday next week.

Lorraine macht sich Gedanken über ihren Geburtstag.
Ergänze in dem folgenden Text die Verben in Klammern in der richtigen Zeit: *simple present*, *will-future*, *going to-future*, *simple past* oder *present perfect*.

What 1 ________ I 1 ____________ (to get) for my 12th birthday next week? Last year I 2 ______________ (to need) a pair of boots, but Mum 3 ______________________ (to buy) me a new pair of shoes. I 4 ____________________ (to need) some new T-shirts every year. Mum always 5 __________________ (to buy) me a new sweatshirt. Perhaps I 6 ______________________________ (to get) a new pair of jeans next week. I hope Mum 7 _________________________________ (to buy) a new skirt for me, too. I'm sure I 8 ____________________________ (to get) some money from my Grandma for my birthday. I 9 ____________________________ (to buy) a new pair of basketball trainers then.

Two weeks later: It was Lorraine's birthday last week.
She wants to buy a new pair of basketball trainers in a sports shop.

Ergänze in dem folgenden Text die Verben in Klammern in der richtigen Zeit: *simple present*, *will-future*, *going to-future*, *simple past* oder *present perfect*.

Shop assistant: "Good afternoon. Can I 1 __________ (to help) you?" • Lorraine: "I 2 __________ (to need) a new pair of trainers. But I 3 ______________________ (not to decide) yet." • Shop assistant: "What size* 4 _________ you 4 _________ (to take)?" • Lorraine: "Normally I 5 ________________ (to take) size 5." • Shop assistant: "6 ______ you ever 6 _________ (to have) a pair of Pike trainers?" • Lorraine: "No, I 7 ____________________ (not to have)." • Shop assistant: "Last week we 8 _________ (to get) the new collection** of trainers. They 9 _______ (to be) very comfortable. I think I 10 ___________________ (to go) and get you a pair of Pike trainers in size 5. Here you are." • Lorraine: "I 11 _____________________ (not to like) the colour. I 12 ________(to buy) a nice pair of trainers here last year." • Shop assistant: "Let me see. Yes, the Lions trainers. But I 13 ____________ (to be) sorry. We 14 ___________________ (not to have got) them any more. We 15 _________ (to sell) the last pair of Lions trainers last week. Perhaps we 16 ___________________ (to get) some new ones next week." • Lorraine: "OK, perhaps I 17 ___________________ (to come) back next week."

* *size* = Größe ** *new collection* = die neuen Modelle

23 A traffic accident

Das Datum von heute

Reading / mixed tenses in questions

Gordon wrote an article about the accident for the Nottingham High School school magazine:

An accident

Susan, an 11 year old girl, went by bike down the High Street.

She was very fast on her new mountain bike.

Suddenly a boy on his skate-board crossed the street.

The boy's name is Shane and he's 11, too.

Susan and Shane both go to Nottingham High School.

They are in the same class and they are friends.

Susan broke her right arm and Shane sprained* his foot and had a big bump on his head.

An ambulance took Susan and Shane to hospital where a doctor x-rayed** Susan's arm and Shane's foot.

They did not go to school for one week. Susan read a lot of comics and Shane played computer games every day. He got a new game for Christmas.

Shane liked it at home with his new computer game. This was his first accident. He loved to have one week with no school.

Susan was very unhappy at home because it has been her second accident this year. In February she had an accident with her bike, too, because the roads were wet and she couldn't brake***.

So, kids, be careful, when you cross a street!

Don't speed with your mountain bikes!!!

* *to sprain* = verstauchen ** *to x-ray* = röntgen *** *to brake* = bremsen

Before Gordon wrote the article, he went to Susan's house and asked her a lot of questions.

Schau dir Susans Antworten an und schreibe dann die Fragen auf, die Gordon gestellt hat. Falls ein Satzteil unterstrichen ist, musst du auch noch das richtige Fragewort finden.

Gordon: "Did you go by bike?" • Susan: "Yes, I went by bike."

Gordon: "____?"

Susan: "Yes, I rode very fast on my mountain bike."

Gordon: "____?"

Susan: "Yes, the boy on the skateboard crossed the street."

Gordon: "____?"

Susan: "Yes, we have been in the same class for a long time."

Gordon: "____?"

Susan: "Yes, we are friends."

Gordon: "____?"

Susan: "The ambulance took us to <u>hospital</u>."

Gordon: "What about Shane?" ______________ ever ______________

______________ before?" • Susan: "No, he has never had an accident before."

Gordon: "____?"

Susan: "No, I will not go to school tomorrow."

Gordon: "Thank you, Susan. I hope you get well soon."

24 A town plan

Das Datum von heute

Prepositions of place

Sieh dir das Bild an.

The car park is behind the supermarket. The bank is opposite the supermarket. There is an envelope on the pavement in front of the post office. The church is next to the post office.

Beschreibe das Bild mit den vorgegebenen Textteilen und benutze dabei die folgenden Präpositionen. Du musst nicht alle benutzen und du kannst auch manche mehrmals benutzen. Schreibe deine Sätze auf ein extra Blatt Papier.

on the right/left – behind – next to – opposite – between – in front of

1. Cinema / school ____________________

2. Church / museum ____________________

3. Pet shop / cinema ____________________

4. Book shop / butcher's shop and post office ____________________

5. Café / tables and chairs ____________________

6. Library / supermarket ____________________

7. Bank-robber / bank ____________________

8. Museum / toy shop ____________________

Spielvorschlag:
Du kannst zusammen mit einem Freund ein Spiel spielen.
Hier sind zwei Vorschläge:

- Stellt euch vor, ihr habt Besuch aus England und müsst eine kleine Führung durch den Ort machen, in dem ihr lebt. Beschreibt eurem Besuch, wo sich was befindet, während ihr mit ihm durch den Ort geht. Schreibt eure Führung kurz auf. Vielleicht braucht ihr sie noch einmal! Kontrolliert eure Präpositionen mit eurem Schulbuch oder einem *dictionary*.
- Ihr habt bestimmt irgendwo einen Stadtplan, oder? Guckt euch zu zweit oder zu dritt den Stadtplan an und beschreibt die Lage der angegebenen Gebäude, Sportanlagen, Kirchen ...
  Am besten legt ihr euer Schulbuch oder ein englisches Wörterbuch bereit, um euch gegenseitig zu kontrollieren.

25 My diary

Das Datum von heute ____________

Prepositions of time

Here is a page from Tim's and Tom's diaries.

Tim December
Monday 21st play football evening
Tuesday 22nd
Wednesday 23rd go swimming with Dad
Thursday 24th CHRISTMAS EVE
Friday 25th **CHRISTMAS DAY** visit Grandma
Saturday 26th 5:00 – 7:00 p. m. theatre play
Sunday 27th go to the sports centre with John, 10:00 a. m.

Tom December
Monday 21st meet Mark at 6:00 p. m.
Tuesday 22nd morning see Doctor Baker
Wednesday 23rd order a pizza
Thursday 24th buy flowers for Mum CHRISTMAS EVE
Friday 25th 9:10 a. m. meet Shane at the station
Saturday 26th have a BOXING DAY-party 6:00 – 10:00 p. m.
Saturday 26th get the new cinema programme

Setze in den Text die angegebenen Präpositionen ein.
Streiche alle benutzten Präpositionen durch.
Eine Präposition bleibt am Ende übrig. Trage sie hier ein: ____________

after – after – after – at – at – at – at – at – before – from – from – in – in – in – in – on – on – on – on – on – on – on – on – past – till – till

Tim and Tom are talking on the phone.
Tim: "771422, Tim Johnson speaking."
Tom: "Hello Tim. It's me, Tom. How are you?"
Tim: "I'm fine. And how are you?"

Tom: "I'm very busy 1 ________ the moment. That's why I'm calling. We wanted to meet this week. But I think it's very difficult. Have you got your diary?" Tim: "Yes, I've got it here." • Tom: "What are you going to do 2 _____ Monday?" Tim: "3 ________ Monday 21st I'm going to play football 4 ________ the evening." Tom: "I'm going to meet Mark 5 ________ 6 o'clock." • Tim: "What about Tuesday morning?" • Tom: "I'm sorry. But I've got an appointment* with Doctor Baker 6 ________ the morning." • Tim: "7 ________ Wednesday, one day 8 ________ Christmas Eve, I'm going go to swimming with Dad and then I'll be busy with my Christmas presents for Mum and Dad. One day 9 ________ Christmas Eve, 10 ________ Christmas day**, we are going to visit Grandma. She lives in London." • Tom: "11 ________ ten 12 ________ nine I'm going to meet Shane at the station 13 ________ Christmas day. Two days 14 ________ Christmas Eve, 15 ________ December 26th, we are going to have a big Christmas party 16 ________ six 17 ________ ten o'clock." • Tim: "18 ________ Boxing Day*** I'm going to see a theatre play 19 ________ five 20 ________ seven o'clock. 21 ________ ten o'clock 22 ________ the morning I'm going to go to the sports centre 23 ________ 27th December." • Tom: "Well, let's meet 24 ________ January 25 ________ Christmas." • Tim: "That's a good idea. I'll call you then. Bye."

* *appointment* = Termin
** *Christmas Day* = erster Weihnachtsfeiertag
*** *Boxing Day* = zweiter Weihnachtsfeiertag

26 At the post office

Das Datum von heute

Word order

Du kannst dich bestimmt noch erinnern: Im Englischen ist die Satzstellung anders als im Deutschen.
Subjekt – Verb – Objekt – Ortsangaben – Zeitangaben
Für besondere Betonungen können die Satzteile auch manchmal an eine andere Position im Satz wandern.

Schreibe die angegebenen Satzteile in der richtigen Satzstellung auf. Denke an die Großschreibung am Satzanfang.

1. to your friends / want to send / do / a letter / you / for Christmas?

   Do you want to send a letter to your friends for Christmas?

2. of December / your letters / should send / you / at the beginning

3. on the front of / the address / should write / you / the envelope

4. the stamp / don't forget / in the right corner / to put

5. want to send / by airmail? / do / it / you

6. an airmail sticker / put / then / on the envelope

Shane will Postkarten verschicken.
Trage die Satzteile unten in der richtigen Satzstellung an der richtigen Stelle des Gesprächs zwischen Shane und dem Postangestellten ein.
Denke an die Großschreibung am Satzanfang.

- [ ] very / you / Thank / much.
- [1] to Germany? / a postcard / How much / is
- [ ] for postcards / need / I / 10 stamps / to Germany. • And / need / for a postcard / I / one stamp / to the USA.
- [ ] please? / Can / put / on / the airmail sticker / you / for me
- [ ] to send / I'd like / it / by airmail. / Yes, • any nice stamps? / Have / got / you

Shane: 1. "How much is ______________________ ?"

Post office clerk: "It's 40 p." • Shane: 2. "______________________

______________________"

Post office clerk: "Here are ten stamps for the postcards to Germany. Do you want to send the postcard to the USA by airmail?"

Shane: 3. "______________________ .

______________________ ?"

Post office clerk: "Yes, I have. You need an air mail sticker, too."

Shane: 4. "______________________ ?"

Post office clerk: Yes, of course.

Shane: 5. "______________________"

27 On the road

Das Datum von heute ____________

Adverbs

Lorraine's big sister Ann has got a new motorbike. It's a Sunday afternoon in winter. The road conditions* are not very good.

* *road conditions* = Straßenverhältnisse

Adjektive beschreiben Personen und Sachen.
Here you see a careful driver with a fantastic car.
adjective noun adjective noun

Adverbien beschreiben Tätigkeiten.
She drives fantastically but carefully.
verb adverb adverb

Die meisten Adverbien bildet man durch das Anhängen von -ly an ein Adjektiv: ***a slow dance – they dance slowly;***
a noisy city – the bus drives noisily; an angry person – he shouts angrily.
Aber es gibt auch unregelmäßige Adverbien, die du lernen musst,
z. B. ***fast*** **und** ***well*****:** ***a fast race – he drives fast; a good driver – he drives well.***

Hier kannst du lesen, wie Lorraines große Schwester mit ihrem neuen Motorrad fährt. An zehn Stellen im Text stehen ein Adjektiv und ein Adverb nebeneinander, aber nur eines ist an jeder Stelle richtig. Du musst an jeder Stelle das falsche Wort durchstreichen. Aus den Buchstaben in Klammern ergibt sich ein Lösungswort. Trage die Buchstaben der Reihe nach unten ein. Los gehts!

First Ann rides through a little village. Here she goes slow (A) / slowly (M). When she goes uphill, her motorbike is very noisy (O) / noisily (B). But then it goes downhill and Ann can go very fast. There is a forest with a lot of high trees. She can't see very good (E) / well (T). So she must drive very careful (H)/ carefully (O). She wants to turn left after the shop. She drives around the corner too quick (O) / quickly (R). There are some cows in the field. There is a dangerous (B) / dangerously (C) railroad crossing.
There is a sign on the road, but she can't read it easy (K) / easily (I) because it's a bit foggy now. Ann tries to brake. But her brakes are very bad (K) / badly (T). A policeman stops her and asks her a lot of questions. Ann answers them nervous (P) / nervously (E). When she stops in front of the red traffic light she is very unhappy (S) / unhappily (G).

Ann is interested in _ _ _ _ _ _ _ _ _ _ .

Übersetze das deutsche Wort in Klammern und trage es in den folgenden Sätzen in der richtigen Form ein: als Adjektiv oder als Adverb.

1. Peter sings ________________ . (gut)

2. She is a ____________________________ piano-player. (wunderbar)

3. She plays ______________________________. (wunderbar)

4. This is a very ____________________________ cow. (hungrig)

28 The British school

Das Datum von heute

Test

Before you can enter the British school you must do the following test.

Bilde Aussagesätze (✔) Negativsätze (✘) oder Fragen (?) im *present perfect* mit den angegeben Satzteilen. (Doppelseite 18, 19, 20)

a) Peter / just / do / his homework (✔)
b) The boys / go / shopping / yet (?)
c) The girls / win / a hockey game / this year (✘)
d) your teacher / give back / the English test (?)
e) My friend and I / be / in town (✔)
f) John / buy / a new exercise book / yet. (✘)

You get 2 points for each correct sentence: "I have _____ points."

Schreibe das Verb in die richtige Zeit ein, im *present perfect* oder *simple past* (Doppelseite 21).

On my way home yesterday I 1 __________ (to see) a big black car." I 2 __________ (not to see) that car in our street before," I 3 __________ (to think). I 4 __________ (to ask) my father but he 5 __________ (not to know) the car. So we 6 __________ (to call) the police. They 7 __________ (to come) at once. "How often 8 __________ you 8 __________ (to see) that car?" 9 __________ (to ask) a policeman. "Two times," I 10 __________ (to say). "Well, somebody 11 __________ (to steal) this car last week. Mr Thomson 12 __________ (to report) it a couple of days ago."

You get 1 point for each correct form: "I have _______ points."

Streiche die falsche Zeitform durch (Doppelseite 18 – 22).

a) I think it is going to rain / will rain.
b) She bought / has bought a new dress yesterday.
c) I haven't done / didn't do my homework yet.
d) When my father was a boy he has played / played hockey at school.

You get 1 point for each correct sentence: "I have ______ points."

Trage die fehlende Präposition ein.

We can meet 1_____ two hours. I'm very busy 2_____ the moment.

Tom's birthday is 3_____ July. Which year was he born 4_____ ?

You get 1 point for each correct preposition: "I have ______ points."

In diesen Sätzen ist entweder das Adjektiv richtig oder das Adverb.
Streiche die falsche Form durch.

a) My father always drives very careful / carefully.
b) Tom spoke very slow / slowly.
c) There was a very angry / angrily police officer.
d) Lorraine plays chess good/well. She's a good / well player.

You get 1 point for each correct sentence: "I have ______ points."

Out of 36 possible points I have altogether ______ points."
Mehr als 27 Punkte? Sehr gut! Herzlichen Glückwunsch! Ein tolles Ergebnis.
Mehr als 22 Punkte? Gut. Die meisten Schwierigkeiten hast du sicher im Griff.
Weniger als 22 Punkte? Du kannst ganz sicher noch ein besseres Ergebnis erreichen! Welche Doppelseiten fandest du besonders schwierig? Schau dir alle Doppelseiten, auf denen du unsicher bist, noch einmal in Ruhe mit dem Lösungsheft an und du wirst ***jeden Tag ein bisschen besser***.
Weniger als 15 Punkte? Dir machen noch zu viele Dinge Schwierigkeiten. Arbeite noch einmal die Doppelseiten 18 — 27 in Ruhe und mit dem Lösungsheft durch. Sicher kann dir auch dein Schulbuch bei deinen Problemen weiterhelfen!

29 Take a break

Das Datum von heute ______

A secret code

A	B	C	D	E	F	G	H	I	J	K	L	M	N	O	P	Q	R	S	T	U	V	W	X	Y	Z
♥	➚	❃	♣	➢	)	✳	➳	✣	❞	✦	●	❍	■	❏	✷	❐	▲	☆	▼	◆	❖	◗	❘	❚	✛

☆ Entschlüssele die geheime Nachricht.

■❏◗ ❚❏◆ ✦■❏◗ ♥ ●❏▼ ❏) ➢■✳●✣☆➳
◗➢●● ♣❏■➢

______

______

☆☆ Kannst du auch verschlüsseln?

WE HAVE YOUR ENGLISH TEACHER: LEAVE ONE THOUSAND POUNDS

______

UNDER THE OLD TREE IN THE PARK

______

A different kind of secret code.

Lies die Anweisung und finde die Wörter.
Die Wörter ergeben einen sinnvollen Satz.
Sie sind in folgende Richtungen geschrieben: → ↓ ↘

1st word starts at H8 and has 5 letters.
2nd word starts at A1 and has 4 letters.
3rd word starts at F6 and has 5 letters.
4th word starts at B1 and has 2 letters.
5th word starts at C4 and has 5 letters.
6th word starts at C10 and has 3 letters.
7th word starts at A6 and has 4 letters.
8th word starts at A2 and has 7 letters.
9th word starts at F5 and has 3 letters.
10th word starts at E3 and has 5 letters.
11th word starts at C8 and has 4 letters.
12th word starts at A4 and has 6 letters.
13th word starts at F1 and has 4 letters.
14th word starts at H1 and has 3 letters.
15th word starts at J9 and has 3 letters.
16th word starts at B12and has 5 letters.
17th word starts at H3 and has 10 letters.

	1	2	3	4	5	6	7	8	9	10	11	12
A	Y	E	P	G	Y	S	I	D	E	D	E	A
B	O	N	J	R	E	T	O	N	M	H	F	L
C	U	G	M	C	A	R	D	S	C	O	N	E
D	R	L	A	E	F	I	M	O	I	P	L	A
E	W	I	O	A	P	E	M	A	T	D	E	R
F	T	S	T	A	T	W	O	R	N	N	E	N
G	A	H	H	R	H	O	T	T	A	R	T	S
H	Y	O	E	V	E	R	Y	W	H	E	R	E
I	C	O	R	N	Y	D	Q	R	S	S	T	S
J	W	E	U	R	T	S	Z	I	C	A	R	S
K	P	L	A	I	S	T	A	T	A	I	N	T
L	W	E	M	T	R	L	M	E	N	P	E	A

Jeden Tag ein bisschen besser

Damit klappt das Lernen spielend! Jedes Heft bietet zu wichtigen schulischen Themen kurze Trainingseinheiten für 15–30 Minuten täglich. So werden die „Denkmuskeln" fit gehalten und das Wissen vertieft. Jedes Heft ist vierfarbig und enthält einen heraustrennbaren Lösungsteil.

Darum ab sofort: **Jeden Tag ein bisschen besser** ...

... im Fach	ISBN 3-589-
Deutsch	
4. Schuljahr	21190-3
5. Schuljahr	21191-1
6. Schuljahr	21193-8
7. Schuljahr	21194-6
8. Schuljahr	21195-4
Übungsdiktate	
4. Schuljahr	21379-2
5. Schuljahr	21243-8
6. Schuljahr	21244-6
7. Schuljahr	21376-0
Für alle Fächer	
Lernen - So geht`s	
5./6. Schuljahr	21373-6
7./8. Schuljahr	21374-4

... im Fach	ISBN 3-589-
Mathematik	
4. Schuljahr	21202-0
5. Schuljahr	21203-9
6. Schuljahr	21204-7
7. Schuljahr	21205-5
8. Schuljahr	21206-3
Testaufgaben	
5. Schuljahr	21355-8
6. Schuljahr	21356-6
Englisch	
5. Schuljahr	21196-2
6. Schuljahr	21197-0
7. Schuljahr	21198-9
8. Schuljahr	21199-7
Französisch	
7. Schuljahr	21168-7

Cornelsen SCRIPTOR

Fragen Sie bitte
in Ihrer Buchhandlung!